Children's FIRST Book of

EARTH AND SPACE

Children's FIRST Book of

EARTH AND SPACE

PARRAGON

Author and Editor
Neil Morris

Projects created by
Ting Morris

Art Direction
Full Steam Ahead Ltd

Designer
Branka Surla

Project Management
Rosie Alexander

Artwork commissioned by
Branka Surla

Picture Research
Rosie Alexander, Kate Miles, Elaine Willis, Yannick Yago

Editorial Assistant
Lynne French

Additional editorial help from
Hilary Bird, Paul Kilgour, Jenny Sharman

Editorial Director
Jim Miles

The publishers would like to thank the following people for their help:
Suzanne Airey, Jenni Cozens, Pat Crisp

First published in 1998

This edition published in 1999 by Parragon

Parragon
Queen Street House, 4 Queen Street,
Bath BA1 1HE

2468109753

Produced by Miles Kelly Publishing Ltd
Bardfield Centre, Great Bardfield, Essex CM7 4SL

ISBN 0-75253-248-0

Printed in Italy

Contents

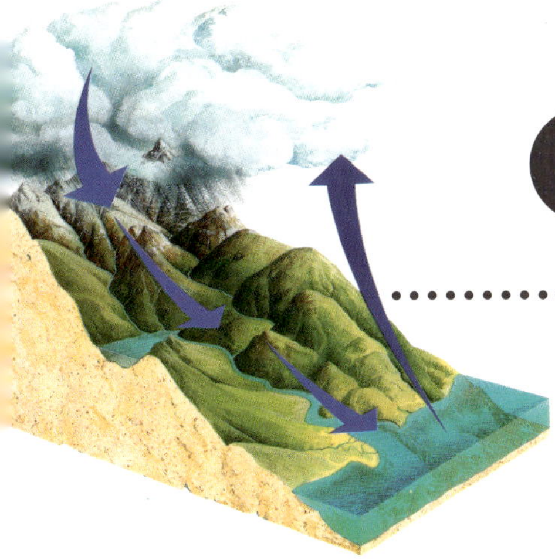

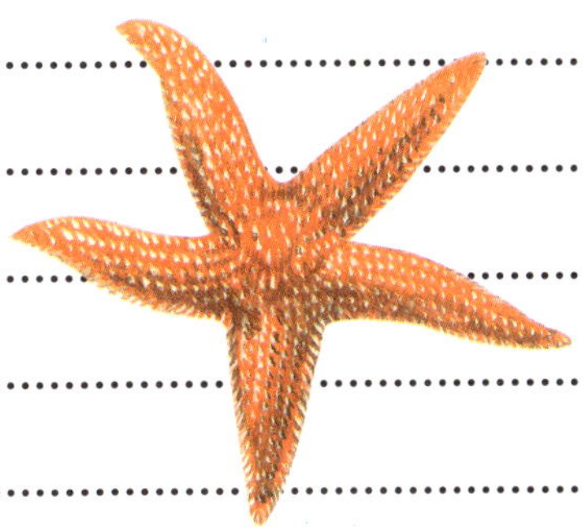

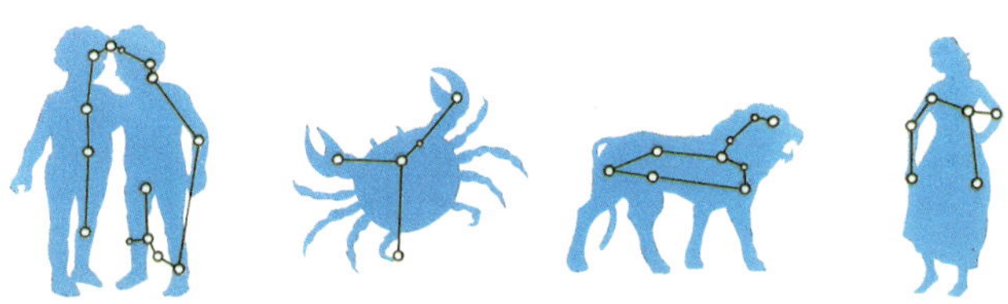

How to use this book

In this book, every page is filled with information on the sort of topics that you will enjoy reading about.

Information is given in photographs and illustrations, as well as in words. All the pictures are explained by captions, to tell you what you are looking at and to give even more detailed facts.

Illustrations are clear and simple, and sometimes they are cut away so that you can see inside things. The triangle at the beginning of the caption text points to the illustration concerned.

Captions beginning with a symbol give extra pieces of information that you will find interesting.

The cartoons throughout the book are not always meant to be taken too seriously! They are supposed to be fun, but the text that goes with them gives real information.

Project boxes describe craft activities related to the topic. These are things to make or simple experiments to do. The photograph helps to show you what to do, and is there to inspire you to have a go! But remember, some of the activities can be quite messy, so put old newspaper down first. Always use round-ended scissors, and ask an adult for help if you are unsure of something or need sharp tools or materials.

The main text on each double-page spread gives a short introduction to that particular topic. Every time you turn the page, you will find a new topic.

Beautiful photographs have been specially chosen to bring each subject to life. The caption triangle points to the right photograph.

A New Words box appears on every double-page spread. This list explains some difficult words and technical terms.

Earth and Space

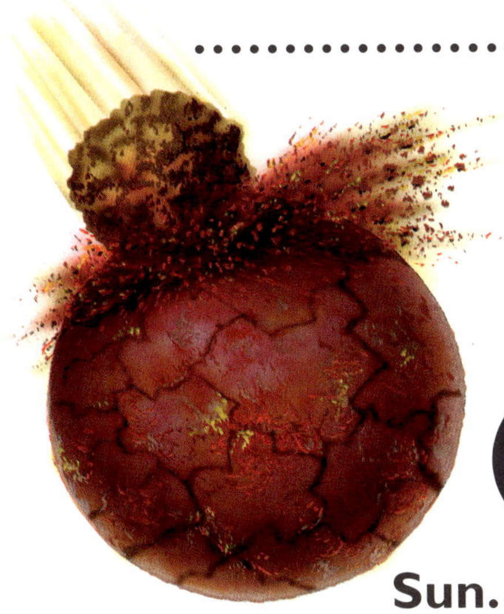

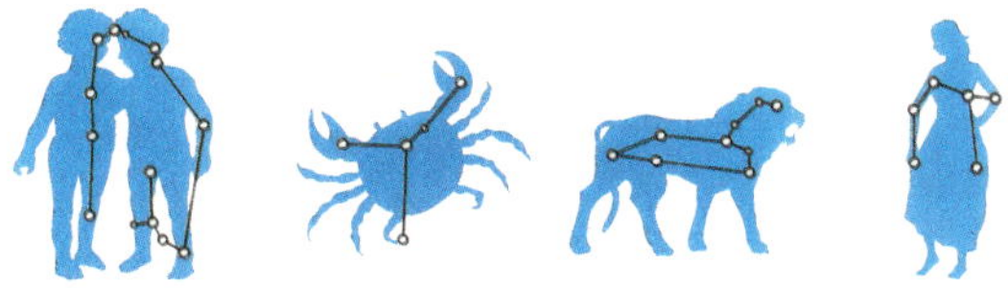

Our home, Earth, is just one of the nine planets that travel around our star, the Sun. And the Sun is really just an ordinary star, like many millions of others in the Universe. Scientists already know an enormous amount about the Universe and space, and yet there is still much more to learn in the future.

On Earth, there are interesting things to see and learn about, from rocky mountains to deep oceans, and from thick forests to sandy deserts. Some of the things we humans do every day are threatening to spoil our planet, but we can all help to make the world a better place.

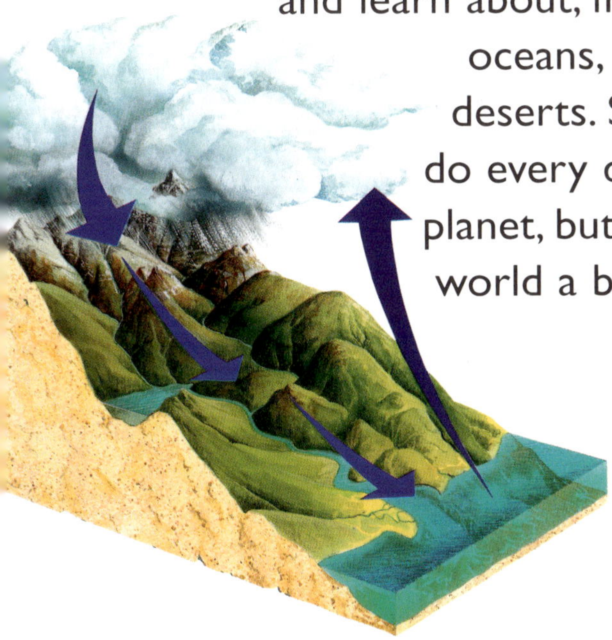

Our Planet

We live on the planet Earth. On our planet there are high mountains and hot deserts, huge oceans and freezing cold regions.

A blanket of air is wrapped around the Earth. This air allows us to breathe and live. Beyond the air, our planet is surrounded by space. A long way away in space, there are other planets and stars. Most planets have satellites, or moons, which circle around them.

△ **From space, Earth** looks like a mainly blue and white planet. It looks blue because water covers most of its surface. The white swirling patterns are clouds, and the brown and green areas are land.

Earth has a diameter of over 12,700 kilometres, almost four times bigger than the Moon. The Moon is about 384,000 kilometres away from Earth.

The Moon circles the Earth once a month. On its journey, different amounts of its sunlit side can be seen from Earth. This makes the Moon seem to change shape during the month.

△ **The Moon spins** as it circles the Earth, so the same side always faces us. People had never seen the other side of the Moon until a spacecraft travelled around it.

New Words

asteroid A miniature planet.

crater A round dent in a planet's surface.

diameter The width of a circle or ball.

satellite A planet that travels around another planet or a star. Earth is a satellite of the Sun.

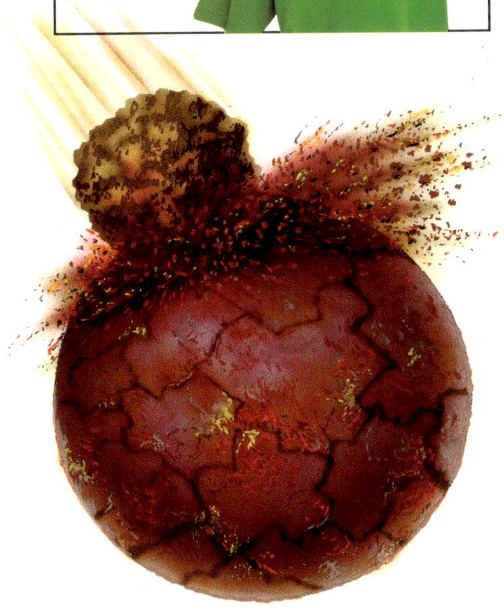

△ **The Moon** was probably formed when a huge asteroid crashed into the Earth billions of years ago. The crash threw rock fragments into space, and these came together to form the Moon.

▷ **The Moon's surface** is full of craters. These were formed by chunks of space rock crashing into it. There is no air or water on the Moon, so it is odd that we call the Moon's vast, dry plains "seas".

The Solar System

Nine planets, including Earth, travel around the Sun. Along with moons, comets and lumps of rock, they make up the Solar System.

This system is Earth's local neighbourhood in space. Everything in it is connected to the Sun by a force that we cannot see. This force is called gravity.

The largest planet, Jupiter, is big enough to hold over 1,300 Earths. The smallest planet, Pluto, is smaller even than our Moon.

▽ **Among the planets** there are four giants – Jupiter, Saturn, Uranus and Neptune. Each has a small rocky core, surrounded by a thick layer of ice or liquid, with gas on the outside. Along with Pluto, these giants are called the outer planets.

PLASTICINE PLANETS

Mould plasticine around beads, marbles and ping-pong balls to make planets. Earth can be blue and white, Mars red and Jupiter orange. Mould a big yellow Sun around a tennis ball. Use black card for a space background and arrange the nine planets in the right order. You could put a label next to each one.

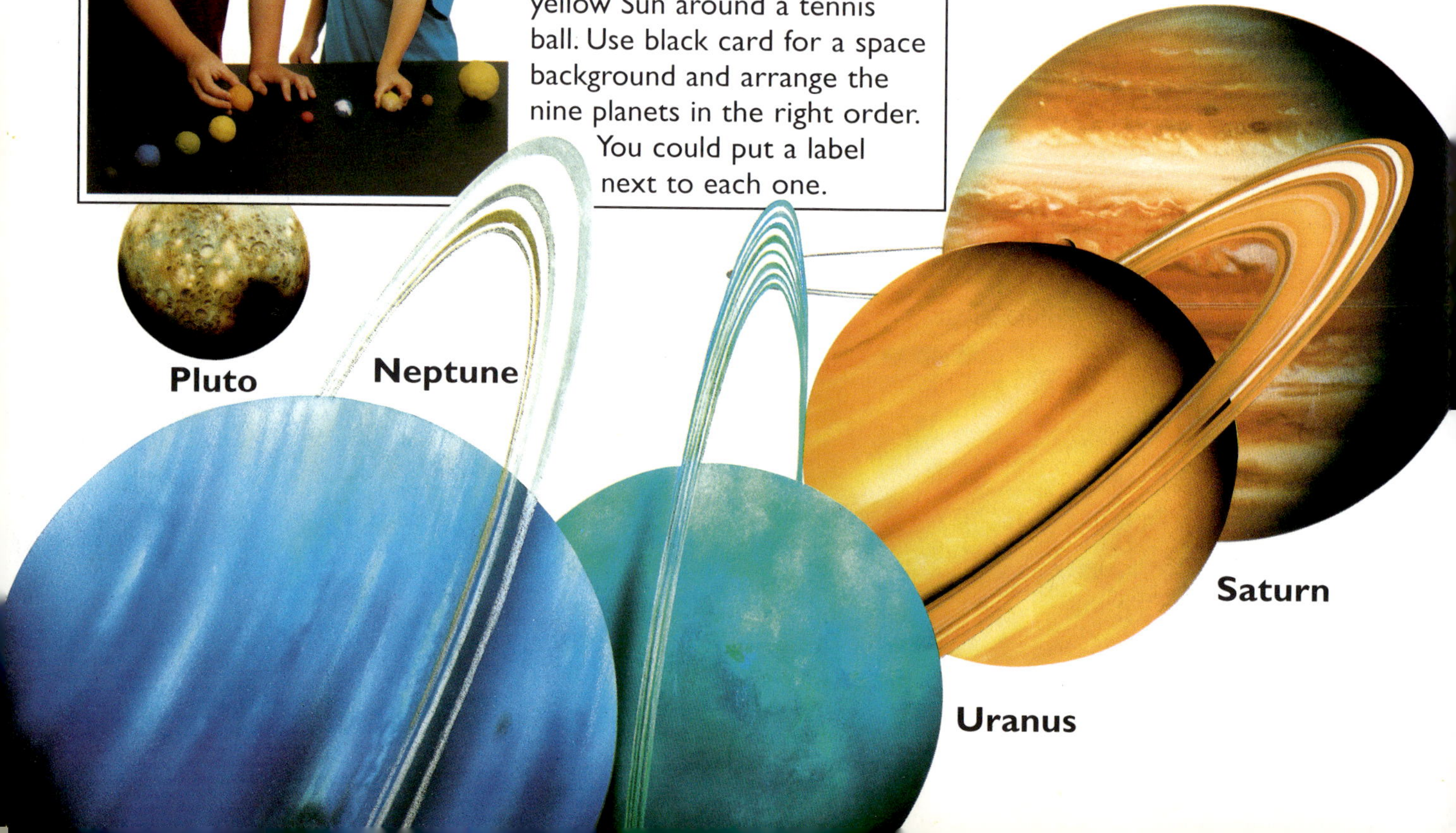

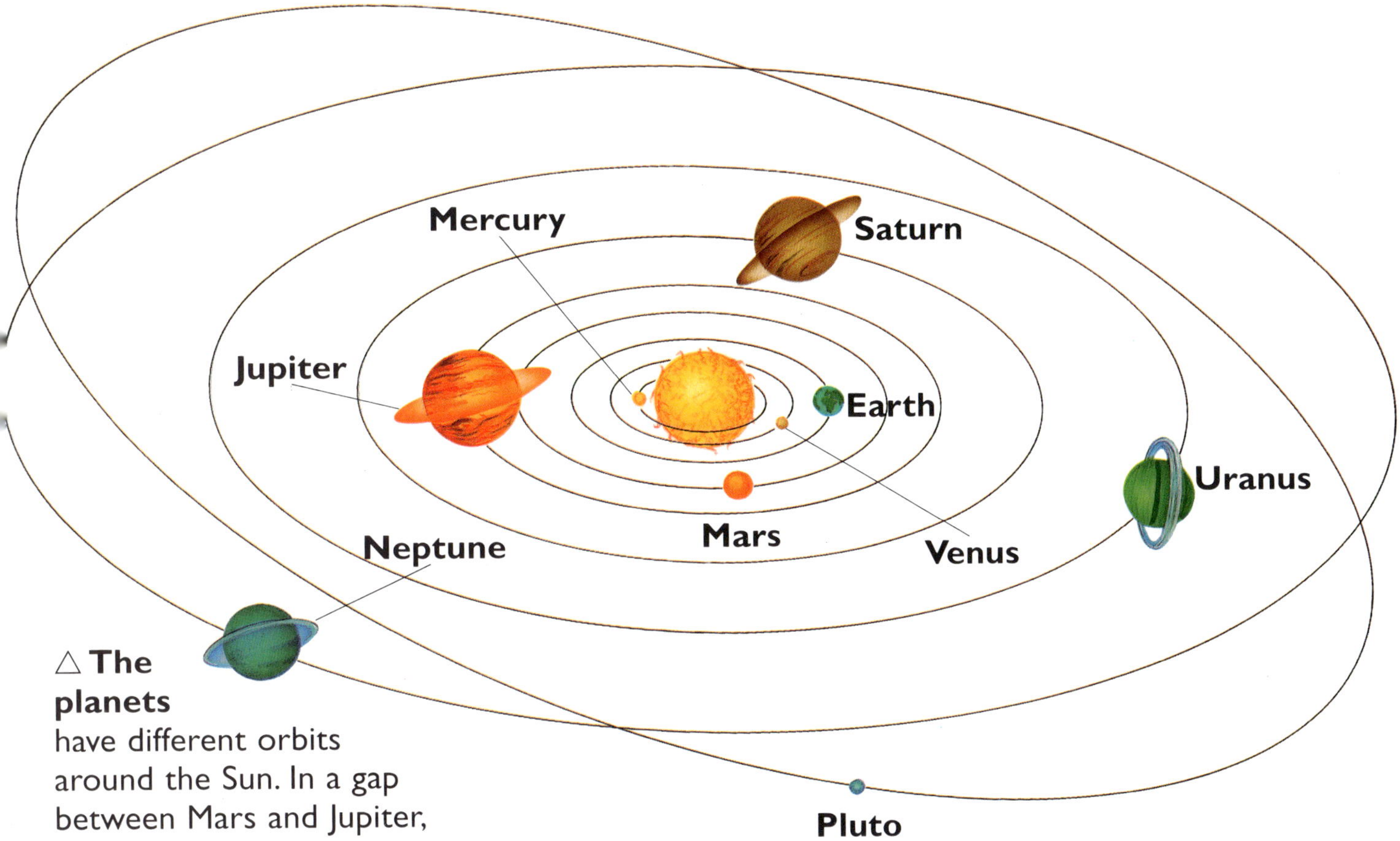

△ **The planets** have different orbits around the Sun. In a gap between Mars and Jupiter, there are thousands of miniature planets, called asteroids. Pluto is usually the furthest planet from the Sun, but sometimes its path crosses Neptune's.

Mercury is a small, rocky planet. It is closest to the Sun and travels around it six times in one of our Earth years.

New Words

comet A snowball of ice and dust that travels around the Sun.

gravity A force that pulls everything towards it.

orbit To travel around something.

solar To do with the Sun.

PLANETS NAMED AFTER GODS

Mercury, messenger of the gods

Venus, goddess of love

Mars, god of war

Jupiter, king of the gods

Saturn, father of Jupiter

Uranus, god of the heavens

Neptune, god of the sea

Pluto, god of the underworld

Our Star

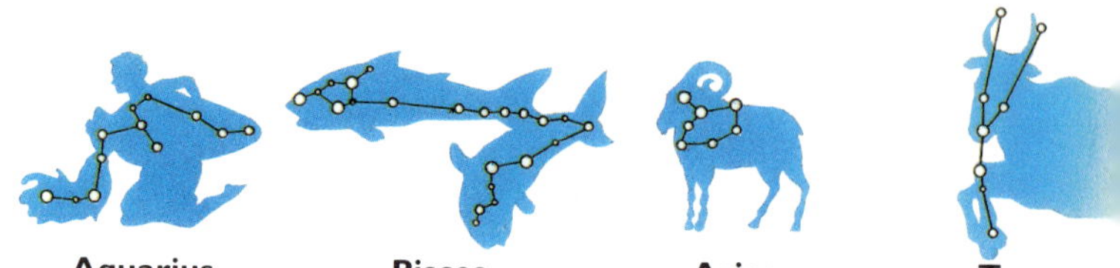

Aquarius, the Water-carrier, 20 Jan-18 Feb

Pisces, the Fish, 19 Feb-20 Mar

Aries, the Ram, 21 Mar-19 Apr

Taurus, the Bull, 20 Apr-20 M

Our Solar System has one star, which we call the Sun. Stars burn, and the sunlight that gives us life is the light of our burning star.

The Sun is a vast, fiery ball of gases. The hottest part of the Sun is its core, where energy is produced. The Sun burns steadily and its energy provides the Earth with heat and light. We could not live without the Sun's light, which takes just over eight minutes to travel through space and reach us.

You must never look directly at the Sun. Its light is so strong that this would harm your eyes.

Twinkle, twinkle, little star
Seen from Earth, stars seem to twinkle. This is because starlight passes through bands of hot and cold air around the Earth, and this makes the light flicker. In space, stars shine steadily.

▷ **Heat from the core** surges up to the Sun's surface, called the photosphere. Sunspots are dark, cooler patches. Prominences are jets of gas that erupt from the surface.

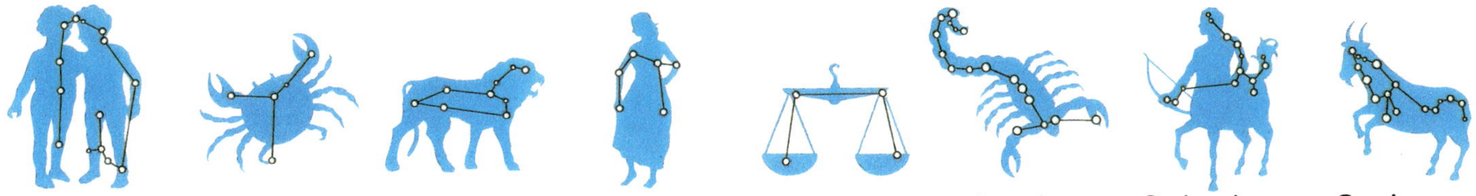

Gemini, the Twins, 21 May-21 June

Cancer, the Crab, 22 June-22 July

Leo, the Lion, 23 July-22 Aug

Virgo, the Virgin, 23 Aug-22 Sept

Libra, the Scales, 23 Sept-23 Oct

Scorpio, the Scorpion, 24 Oct-21 Nov

Sagittarius, the Archer, 22 Nov-21 Dec

Capricorn, the Goat, 22 Dec-19 Jan

△ **Stars seem** to form patterns in the sky. Ancient peoples made pictures of them and gave them names. The constellations of the zodiac are used in horoscopes.

NEW WORDS

constellation A group of stars that form a pattern.

energy The ability to do work.

galaxy A very large group of stars.

horoscope A forecast of things that will happen in the future.

photosphere The surface of the Sun.

▽ **Stars cluster together** in groups called galaxies. The Sun is just one of billions of stars in our galaxy, which is called the Milky Way. It got its name because, from Earth, it looks like a creamy band of stars across the sky.

▷ **Millions of years** after the Big Bang, gases clustered into clouds. These clouds clumped together to form galaxies.

The planets formed later from clouds of gas, dust and rocks. As the Universe expands, the galaxies are moving further apart.

△ **There are countless** billions of stars in the Universe. Sometimes a very old star explodes. We call this a supernova. New stars are being created all the time in different sizes.

▽ **The Sun** is an ordinary yellow star. It is much bigger than a red dwarf star, which is half as hot. A blue giant is at least four times hotter than the Sun. A red supergiant is five hundred times the Sun's width.

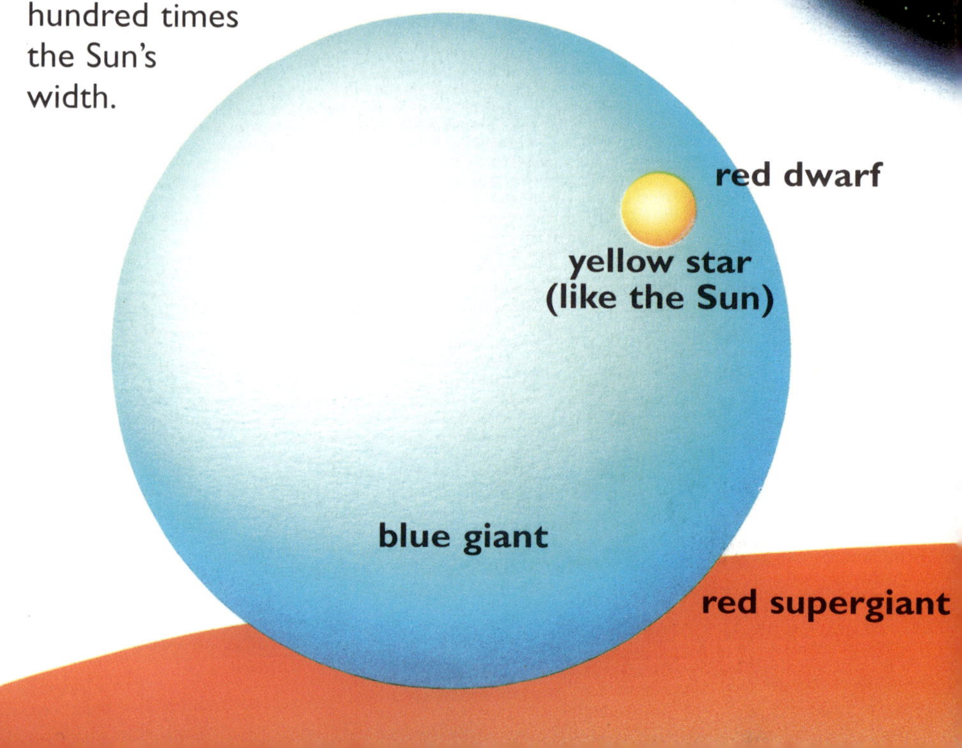

New Words

expand To become larger.

scientist A person who studies the way things work.

supernova A very old star when it explodes.

The Universe

Our address in space is "Earth, Solar System, Milky Way Galaxy, Universe". The Universe is the biggest thing there is and includes all the empty parts of space between the stars.

Most scientists think that the Universe began with a big bang, which happened billions of years ago. Since then it has been growing bigger and bigger in all directions, creating more and more space.

UNIVERSAL BALLOON

Paint white, squiggly, galaxy shapes on a large blue balloon. Let the paint dry, and then slowly blow up the balloon. You will see the galaxies moving apart on the balloon, just as they are doing in the Universe.

Days and Seasons

As the Earth travels around the Sun, it spins like a top. It turns right round once every 24 hours, and this gives us day and night.

The part of the Earth facing the Sun is in daylight. When that part turns away from the Sun, it gets dark and has night-time.

We have seasons because the Earth has a tilt, so that north and south are not straight up and down. When the northern half of the Earth is tilted towards the Sun, it is summer there. At that time it is winter in the southern half of the world, because it is tilted away from the Sun's warmth.

NEW WORDS

equator
An imaginary line around the middle of the Earth.

landscape The way the surface of the Earth looks.

season
One of the four main parts of the year – spring, summer, autumn and winter.

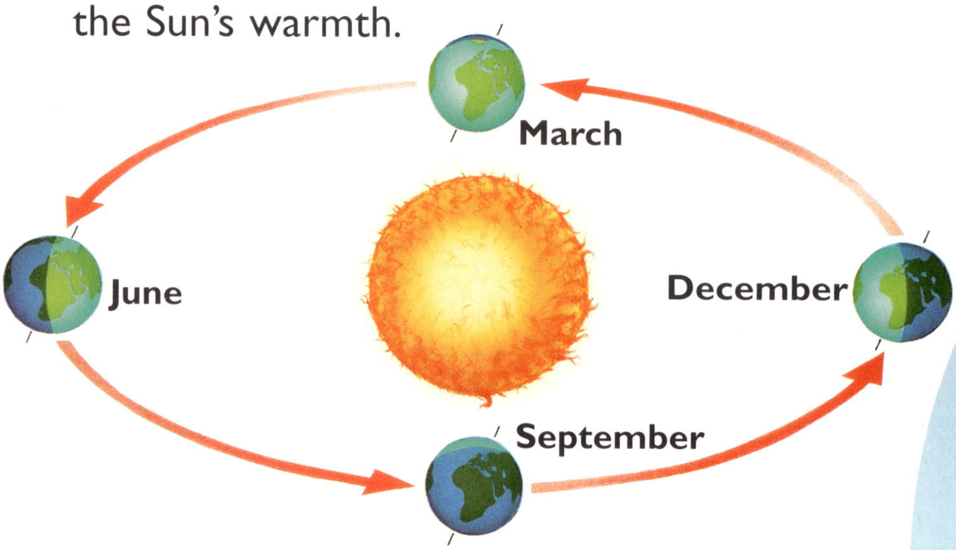

△ **In June** the northern part of the Earth is tilted towards the Sun. It is summer there then, with long, light days and short, dark nights. In December it is the exact opposite. Then the Sun shines more directly on the southern part and makes it warmer.

It takes a year for the Earth to travel all the way around the Sun. During that time the Earth spins round 365 times, giving that number of days. At the same time the Moon travels around the Earth 12 times, giving that number of months.

spring

NIGHT AND DAY

In a darkened room, shine a torch at a globe of the Earth. If you haven't got a globe, use a large ball. The globe or ball is the Earth, and your torch acts like the Sun as it shines on our planet. The side facing the Sun gets light, so there it is day. On the dark side of the globe it is night. You could slowly spin the Earth round, to see how day and night follow each other around the globe.

In some places around the middle of the Earth, near the equator, there are only two seasons. One part of the year is hot and dry, and the other part is warm and wet.

▽ **The Earth's landscape** changes with the seasons. Many trees grow new leaves in spring. The leaves are green and fully grown in summer. They turn brown and start to fall in autumn. In winter, the trees' branches are bare.

winter

summer

autumn

Looking at the Sky

Since ancient times, people have learned a lot about the Universe by studying the night sky.

Early astronomers simply used their naked eyes. Modern astronomers look through big, powerful telescopes so that they can see planets and stars close up. Today, there is even a telescope out in space, which sends pictures back to Earth.

△ **The sighting of a comet** is an exciting event. Comets are huge snowballs made of ice and dust. When they come close to the Sun, they develop tails of gas and dust that may be many hundreds of thousands of kilometres long.

New Words

astronomer A person who studies the stars, planets and space.

observatory A building with a big telescope for looking at the stars and planets.

telescope An instrument you look through to make faraway things look bigger.

Astronomers look at the dark night sky. In the daytime, the sky is lit up by the Sun. This strong light makes it impossible to see other stars.

▷ **Big telescopes** are usually housed in observatories. These are dome-shaped buildings, with a roof that can slide open to show part of the sky. The best observatories are on mountain tops, well away from city lights, giving clear views of the sky above.

Copernicus

Galileo

Newton

Hubble

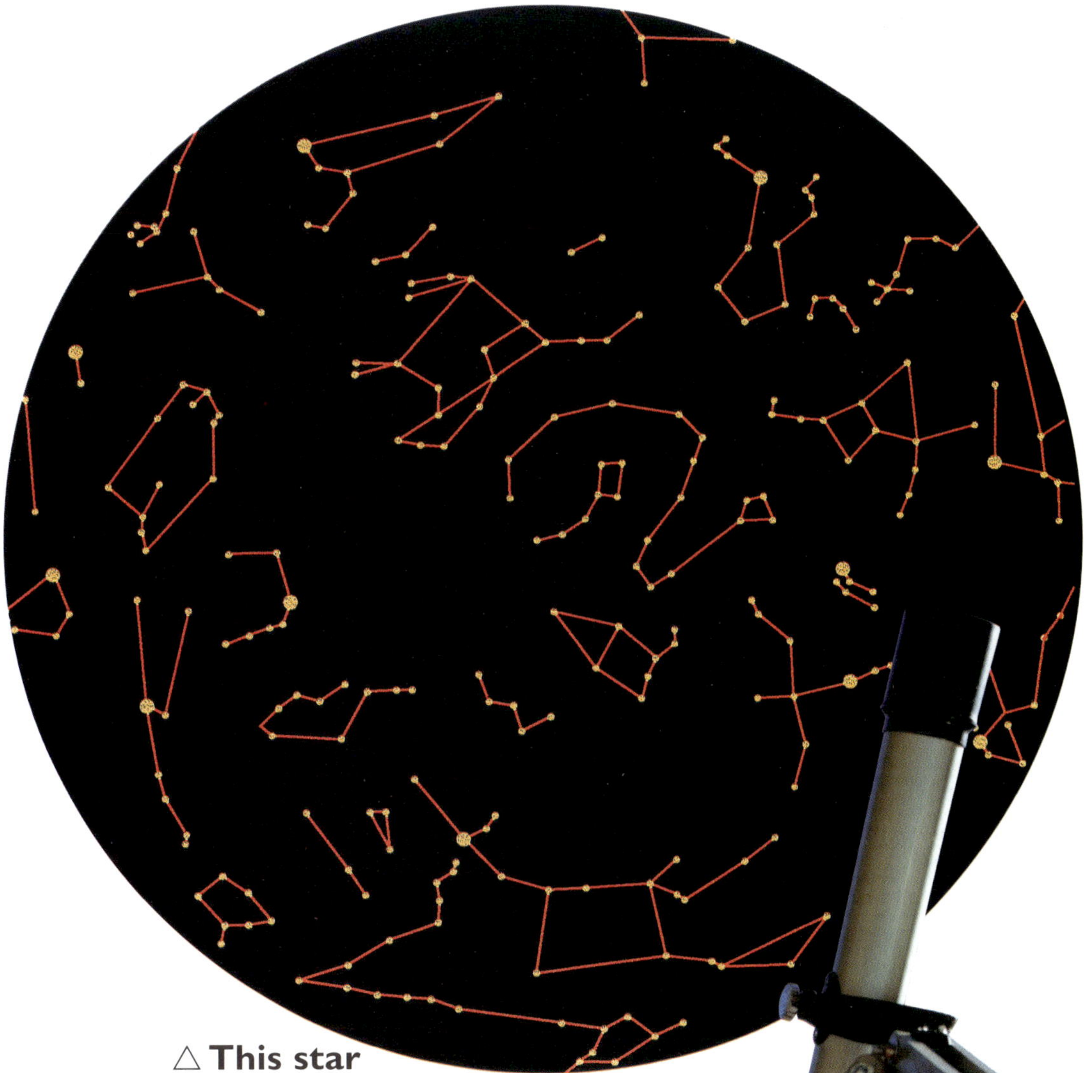

△ **This star map** shows all the stars you can see in a year if you live in the northern half of the world. The stars have been joined together to make constellation patterns. People who live in the southern half of the Earth see different patterns.

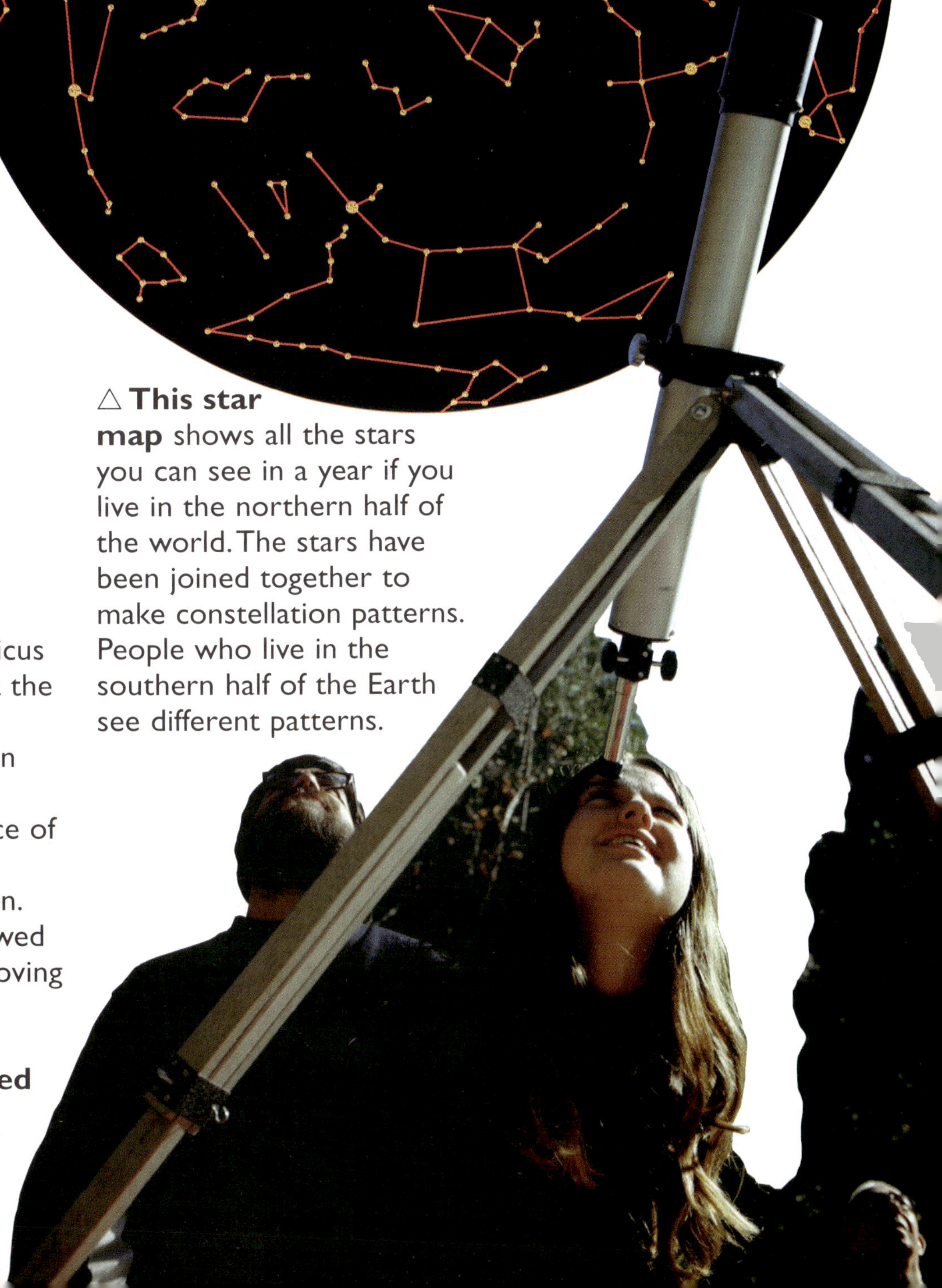

△ **Four famous astronomers**. Copernicus was the first to say that the Earth circles the Sun. Galileo designed his own telescope. Newton discovered that the force of gravity keeps the Earth travelling around the Sun. Hubble's telescope showed him that galaxies are moving steadily apart.

▷ **If you are interested** in studying the sky, you could join your local astronomical society.

Travelling in Space

Spacecraft are blasted into space by powerful rockets. Once the rocket has used up its fuel, the spacecraft carries on under its own power.

Astronauts are space travellers. They live and work in space, sometimes for months on end. Astronauts have to do special training, because there is so little gravity in space. This means that everything in a spacecraft floats about, including the astronauts.

▷ **The space shuttle** is a reusable spacecraft. It rides on a huge fuel tank to take off, uses its own power in space, and lands back on Earth like a plane. Shuttles are used to take astronauts up to space stations.

◁ **In 1969,** American astronauts visited the Moon for the first time. They landed in a lunar module and wore spacesuits to walk on the Moon's surface. The suits protected them, provided them with air to breathe and kept them at the right temperature.

The first living thing to travel in space was a dog named Laika, in 1957. On April 12, 1961, Russian Yuri Gagarin circled the Earth once to become the first person in space. Just a few weeks later, Alan Shepard became the first American astronaut. His space flight lasted just about 15 minutes.

▷ **Astronauts can travel** a short distance away from their spacecraft by putting a special jet-unit on their back. They can move or turn in any direction with this Manned Manoeuvring Unit attached to them.

New Words

astronaut A person who travels in space.

lunar module The part of a spaceship that lands on the Moon.

magnetic Able to stick to metal objects by the power of magnetism.

space station A spaceship in which astronauts can live and work.

What do astronauts eat?
Most space food is dried, to save weight. Water is added to the food packets before they are heated. Astronauts have to hold on to their food, otherwise it just floats around the spacecraft. All knives and forks are magnetic, so that they stick to the meal trays.

The Atmosphere

New Words

atmosphere The gases around a planet. Its thickness depends on the amount of gas.

radiation Tiny particles given out by a star or planet.

tornado A whirlwind storm.

weather Conditions such as rain, snow, wind or sunshine.

The Earth is surrounded by a blanket of air, called the atmosphere. Air is very important: without it, there would be no rain, in fact no weather, and no life.

The atmosphere is made up of many gases, including nitrogen and oxygen. We need to breathe oxygen to stay alive. High up in the atmosphere, a gas called ozone provides a barrier to harmful radiation from the Sun.

Mars has an atmosphere a hundred times thinner than Earth's. Mercury has almost no atmosphere at all.

▽ **The higher you go,** the less air there is. This can create problems for mountaineers. When they need to use a lot of energy at great heights, they sometimes wear oxygen masks.

▷ **Wind** is moving air. Sometimes whirling winds form a spinning funnel of air called a tornado. These extreme winds can destroy anything in their path.

◁ **The atmosphere** is made up of several layers. We live in the bottom layer, the troposphere, which is up to 20 kilometres thick. The furthest layer away, the exosphere, has very little gas.

HEAVY AIR

Tie two balloons to the ends of a stick. Hang the stick from a piece of string so that it balances. Then blow up one of the balloons, and try to balance the stick again. You'll find it won't balance properly, because the air in the blown-up balloon makes it weigh more and so pushes that end down. This simple experiment shows that air has weight.

PLANET EARTH PUZZLE

Place a piece of tracing paper on the map at the bottom of this page. Trace the thick lines of the plates with a black felt pen, and add the outlines of the continents in pencil. Then stick the traced map onto card and colour it in. Cut the map up into separate pieces to make your jigsaw. Jumble up the pieces, then use the plate lines to help you fit your jigsaw together again.

The Earth's crust is cracked into huge pieces that fit together like a giant jigsaw puzzle. These pieces are called plates. The Earth's oceans and continents are split up by the plates, which float on the mantle.

▽ **Earth** looks cool from space, because of its water. Inside, it is incredibly hot. It is over 6,000 km from Earth's surface to its centre.

NEW WORDS

continent A huge land mass.

core The central part of the Earth.

crust The Earth's outer shell.

mantle A thick layer of hot rock.

molten Melted, or turned into hot liquid.

plate A piece of the Earth's crust.

Inside the Earth

Our planet Earth is a large ball of rock and metal, covered with water and soil.

The Earth is made up of four layers. The thin outer layer, called the crust, is the Earth's skin – rather like the peel of an orange. Beneath the crust is a thick layer, called the mantle, which is made of hot, molten rock.

Near the centre of the Earth are the two layers of the planet's core, which is made of metal.

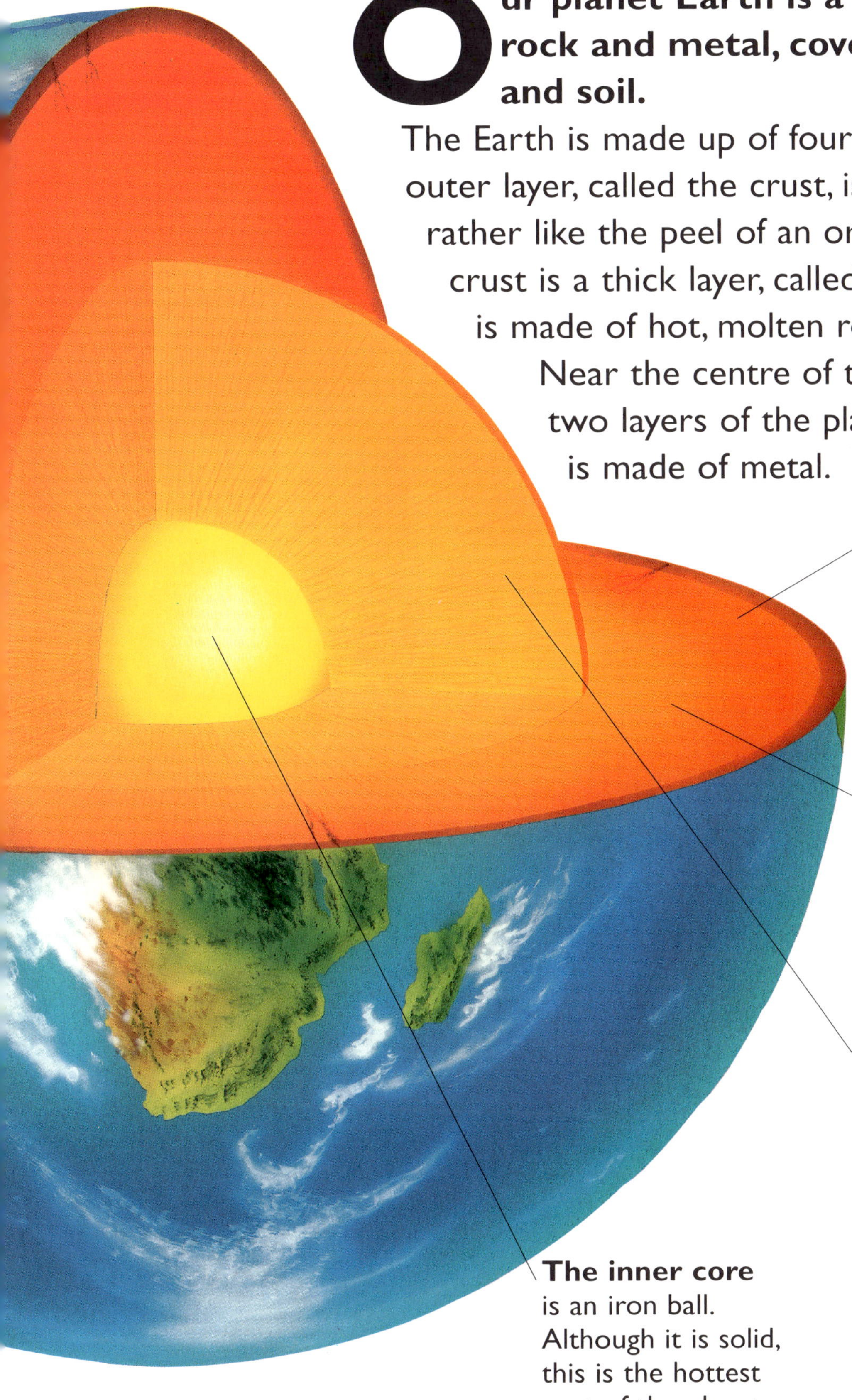

Volcanoes and Earthquakes

△ **The San Andreas Fault**, in California, shows where two of the Earth's plates slide past each other. They move about 5 centimetres a year.

The plates that make up the Earth's crust slowly move and rub against each other. Though they only move a few centimetres each year, their buckling can cause volcanoes and earthquakes.

Volcanoes and earthquakes usually form near the edge of plates. Many of them happen in a region around the Pacific Ocean called the "Ring of Fire". They sometimes cause giant waves called tsunamis.

The strongest recorded earthquake happened in Ecuador in 1906. It measured 8.6 on the Richter scale, which is used to measure the strength of earthquakes. In 1995, an earthquake at Kobe, in Japan, killed 5,500 people and damaged 190,000 buildings.

◁ **Flyovers and bridges** are at great risk when they are shaken by an earthquake. The quake's waves move out from a point called the epicentre. Very often there are minor tremors before and after a big earthquake.

The world's largest active volcano is Mauna Loa, in Hawaii. It rises to 4,170 metres above sea level, and is over 9,000 metres high when measured from the ocean bed. It usually erupts about once every four years.

Shaken but not damaged?
The 48-storey Transamerica Pyramid is San Francisco's tallest building, at 260 metres high. It was specially designed to be able to survive earthquakes. Scientists and designers are always looking for new ways to make tall buildings safer for people.

A volcano that has not erupted for a long time is called dormant, or "sleeping". If a volcano has done nothing at all for thousands of years, it is said to be extinct.

▽ **When a volcano** erupts, red-hot lava blasts up through an opening in the Earth's crust. The steep sides of a volcano mountain are made of layers of hardened lava and ash. These layers build up with each eruption.

New Words

epicentre The centre of an earthquake, where the shaking waves come from.

lava Melted rock that flows from a volcano.

tremor A shaking movement.

tsunami A giant wave that can cause great damage.

Water

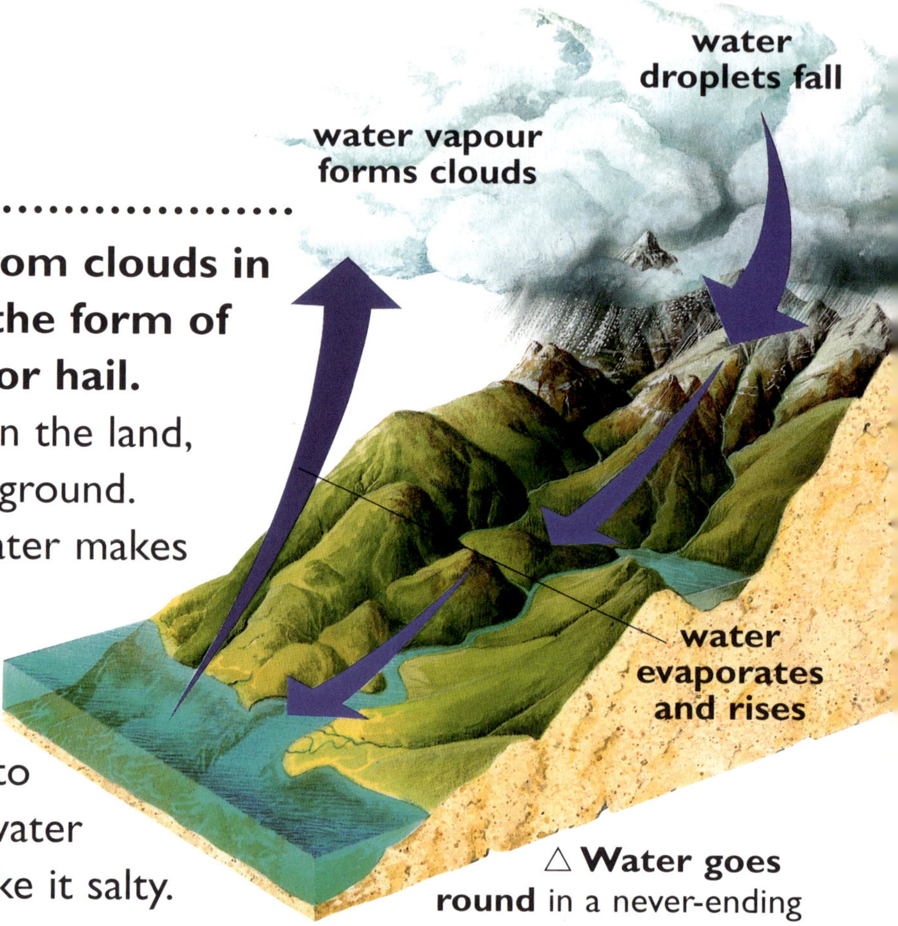

Water falls from clouds in the sky in the form of rain, snow or hail.

When rainwater falls on the land, some of it seeps into the ground. In limestone areas, this water makes underground caves. Some water collects in lakes, but most forms rivers that finally find their way to the sea. On the way, the water picks up minerals that make it salty.

△ **Water goes round** in a never-ending cycle. First, it evaporates from the oceans. The water vapour rises and turns into clouds. When the droplets in the clouds get too heavy, they fall to land as rain. Some rain flows back to the oceans, and then the water cycle starts all over again.

MEASURING RAIN

To make your own rain gauge, use an empty jam jar. Pour in 200 ml of water, 10 ml at a time. Use a permanent marker to mark 10-ml levels on the jar. Empty the jar and put in a funnel. Then put your gauge outside to catch the rain.

NEW WORDS

cave An underground tunnel.

evaporate To turn into a vapour or gas.

gauge An instrument that measures something.

limestone A soft kind of rock.

mineral A hard substance that is usually found in the ground in rock form.

In caves, minerals in dripping water make stalactites. These hang down from the roof of the cave, while stalagmites grow up from the ground. Sometimes they meet up to form a column.

◁ **Most underground caves** are made by running water. Over many years, rainwater wears away at cracks in soft limestone rocks. The cracks grow wider, making holes and then wide passages. Constantly dripping water creates fantastic rock shapes inside caves.

▷ **Where a river** drops over the edge of a hard rockface, it becomes a waterfall. Victoria Falls plunges 108 metres on the Zambezi River in Africa.

▽ **This cross-section** shows how water wears away limestone rocks and hollows out caves. The stream on the surface drops into a sinkhole and forms a shaft.

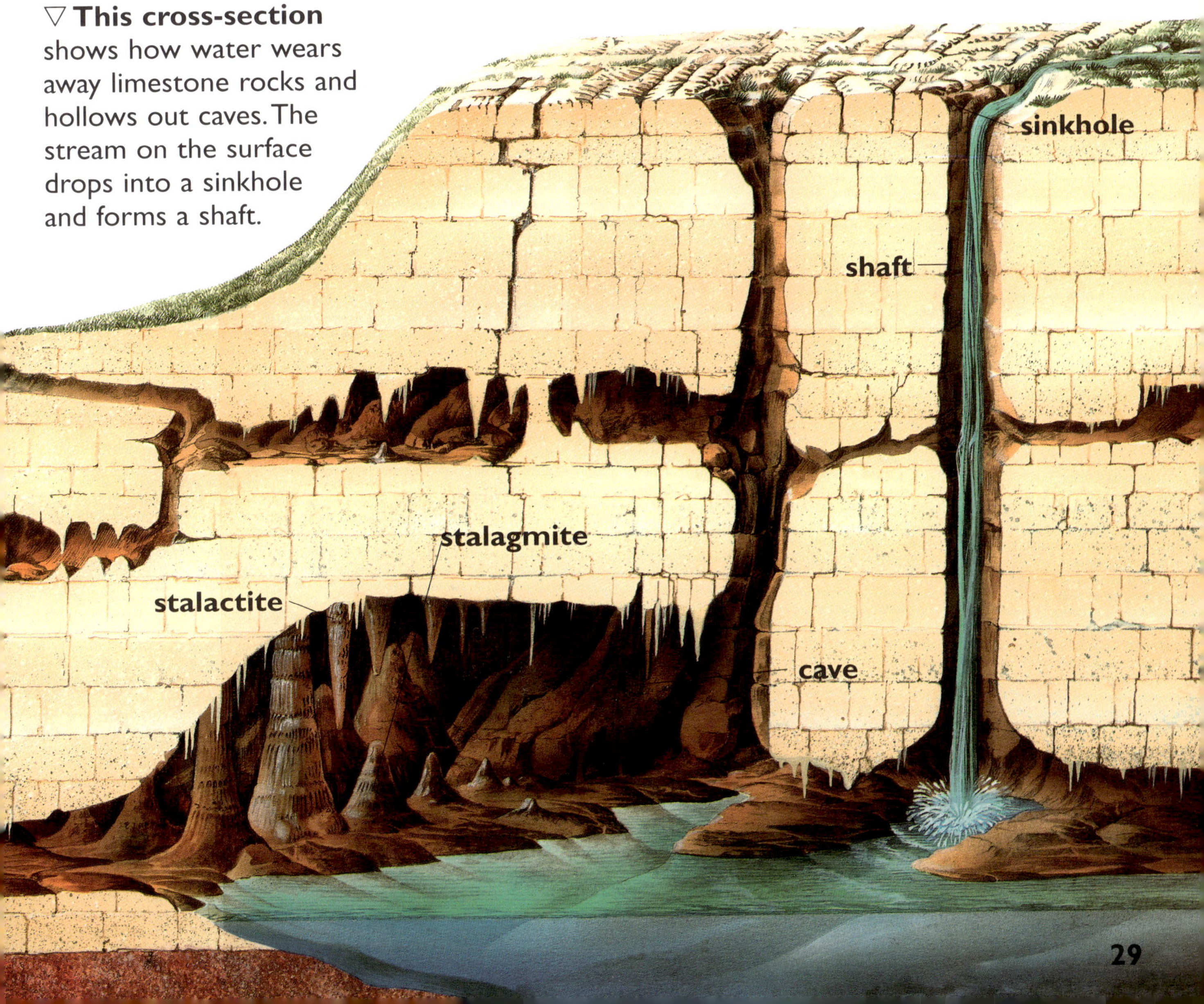

SEA OF ISLANDS

Collect some stones and stick them together with plasticine. Put your plasticine mountains in a plastic bowl and pour water in. As the bowl fills with water, islands form. It is easy to see that small islands are really the tops of underwater mountains. How many islands have you made?

△ **Viewed from space**, the Earth looks like a very watery planet. The Pacific Ocean covers almost half the surface of the globe.

The land to the bottom left of the ocean is Australia. At the top left is Russia, and at the top right is the North American continent.

New Words

coral reef A ridge formed by the skeletons of tiny sea creatures.

globe The round ball shape of the Earth.

trench A valley on the sea bed.

◁ **This sea fan** is a type of coral. Coral reefs usually form in the shallow waters around warm land. They are home to thousands of colourful plants and animals. The biggest coral reef in the world is the Great Barrier Reef, off the coast of Australia.

Land and Sea

Millions of years ago, the Earth's land was made up of a single, huge continent. One big, deep ocean covered the rest of the planet.

Over millions of years, the original land mass split itself up into large pieces. As these pieces gradually moved further apart, the Atlantic, Indian and Arctic Oceans were formed. Today we call the remains of the huge stretch of water the Pacific Ocean.

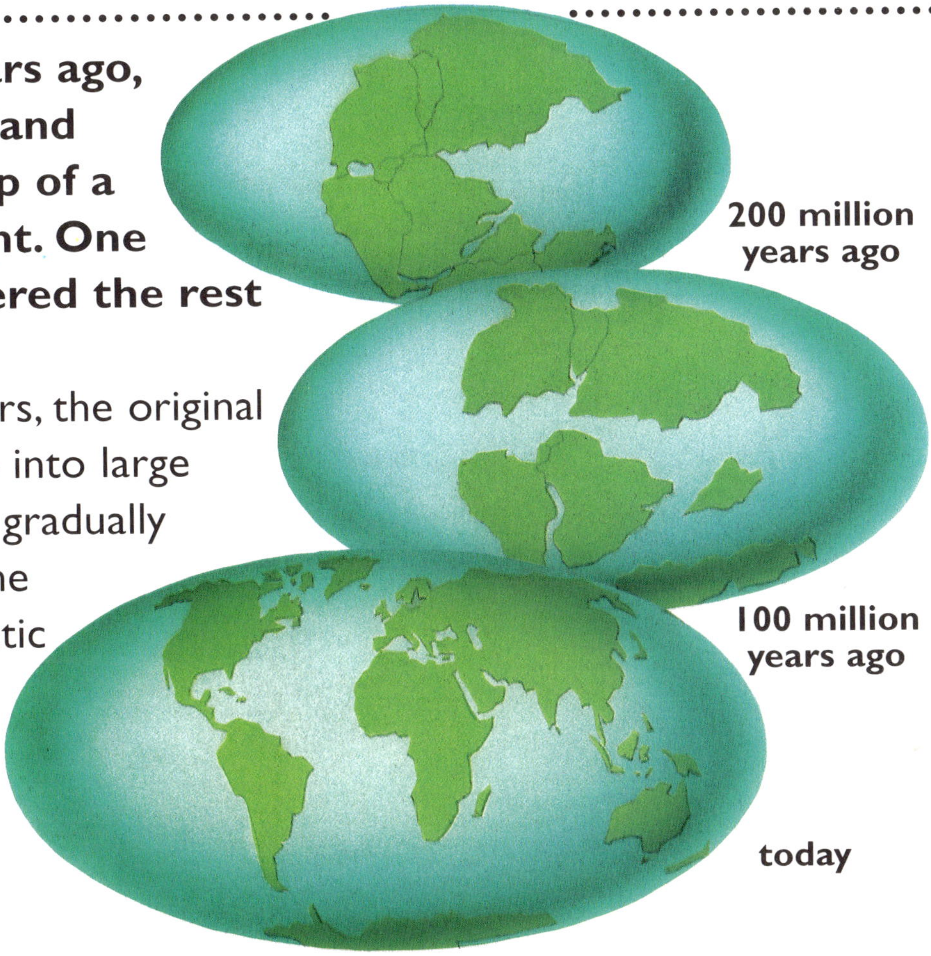

▽ **The ocean floor** has many similar features to dry land. There are mountains called seamounts and guyots, and valleys called trenches. A mid-ocean ridge is where new rock is made from molten rock below.

The continents, in order of size, are: Asia, Africa, North America, South America, Antarctica, Europe and Australasia. Together, they cover less of the Earth's surface than the Pacific Ocean.

△ **The continents were** once joined together as a giant supercontinent, called Pangaea. This split into two land masses, and eventually separate continents formed. The continents are still moving apart, very slowly.

At the Seashore

Where an ocean meets land, waves pound against the shore. This wears away at the rocks, in a process called erosion.

Oceans carve the shapes of the world's coastlines. Cliffs of soft rock, such as white chalk, are worn away more quickly than hard rock. Waves grind rocks down into pebbles and sand, and they move about as waves break on the seashore.

Twice a day, the water in oceans rises and goes down again. The tides are caused by the pull from the gravity of the Moon and the Sun.

New Words

☆**erosion** Wearing something away.
☆**pinnacle** A pointed pillar or peak.
☆**shellfish** A type of sea creature that has a shell to live in.
☆**tide** The rise and fall in the level of the sea that happens twice a day.

▽ **Coasts** sometimes wear away to make strange shapes. As the oceans break down a cliff face, rocky pinnacles may be left. As they wear away further, the pinnacles eventually collapse.

screw shell

strawberry top

spider conch

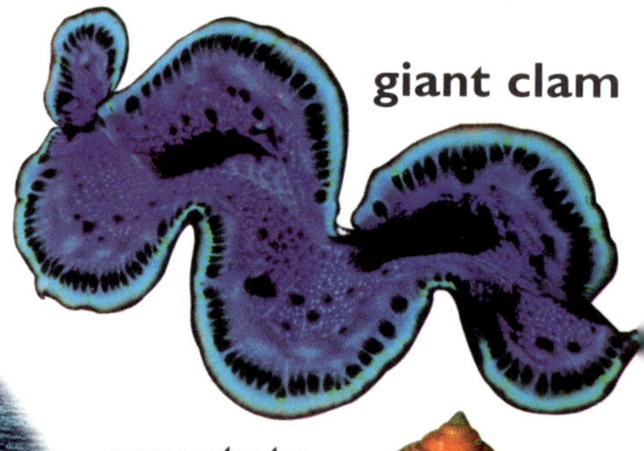

giant clam

punctate maurea

△ **On rocky shores,** shellfish hide in their shells until the tide rolls in. The giant clam has the largest shell. It can grow up to 1.5 metres across.

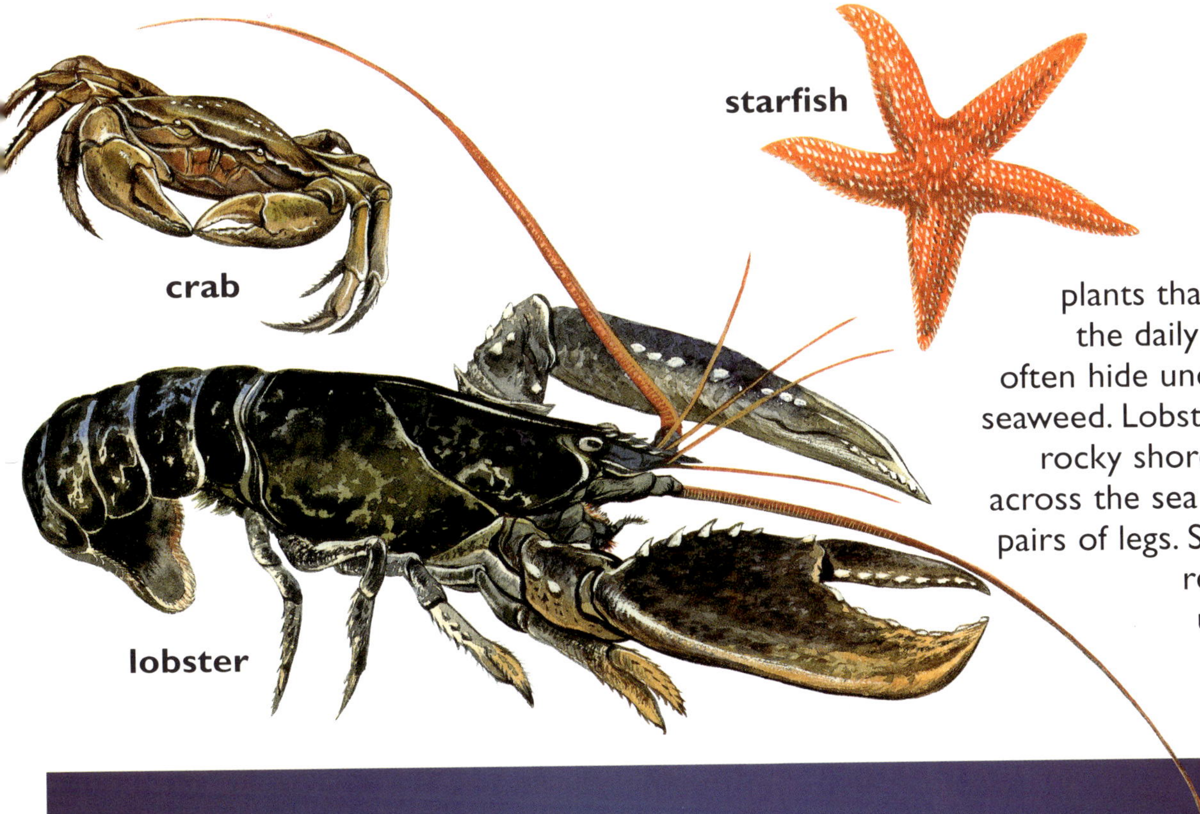

◁ **The seashore** teems with animals and plants that depend on the daily tides. Crabs often hide under rocks or seaweed. Lobsters live near rocky shores and move across the sea bed on four pairs of legs. Starfishes are related to sea urchins. They usually have five arms.

△ **Beautiful sandy beaches,** like this one on a Caribbean island, are a great favourite with holidaymakers all over the world. We don't think of these beaches as rocky, but grains of sand are really just very tiny pieces of broken rock and shells. Sand is popular with shellfish and other shore creatures too, because it is easy for them to dig into.

Lugworms make the coiled tubes of sand that we sometimes see on the shore. The worms dig under the beach, eating the sand for the tiny creatures that live in it.

The world's biggest tides are found in the Bay of Fundy, in the Atlantic Ocean off Canada. There is up to 14.5 metres between high and low tides.

Why are pebbles smooth?

Big rocks break away from the land and fall into the sea. The rocks break up into smaller pebbles, and these knock against each other. Eventually they are worn smooth by being dragged up and down the shore by waves.

Mountains

There are high mountains all over the world. They took millions of years to form, as the plates that make up the Earth's crust squeezed and buckled.

Mountain ranges that lie near the edge of plates are still being pushed higher. They have steep, rocky peaks. Older ranges that lie further from the plate edges have been worn away over the years by rain, wind and ice.

It is cold on high mountains, and the peaks have no plants.

New Words

- **crag** A steep piece of rough rock.
- **range** A group or series of mountains.
- **strata** Layers of rock.

△ **The Earth's plates** are made up of layers of rock, called strata. As the plates move, the strata are bent into folds. In the mountains, you can often see how the layers have been folded into wavy lines.

▷ **The longest** mountain range on land is the Andes, which stretches for over 7,000 kilometres down the west coast of South America. The Transantarctic Mountains stretch right across the frozen continent of Antarctica.

△ **Block mountains** are created when the Earth's crust develops cracks, called faults, and the chunk of land between them is pushed up.

△ **Dome mountains** form when the top layers of the Earth's crust are pushed up by molten rock underneath. This makes a big bulge.

△ **Fold mountains** are formed when one plate bumps and pushes against another. Rock is squeezed up into folds. The Andes were made this way.

Mountains are often joined together in a series, or range. The longest and highest ranges, such as the Andes and the Himalayas, form huge mountain systems. Few animals or people live on the highest mountains.

MOUNTAINS OF JUNK

Crumple newspaper into big balls and tape them onto a cardboard base. Make papier-mâché pulp by soaking newspaper pieces in a bucket of wallpaper paste. Cover the balls with the pulp to make mountains and valleys. When your landscape is dry, paint some snow-capped peaks with white paint. Sprinkle the base with sand and grit. You could add a mountain lake.

What is an ibex?

The ibex is a wild mountain goat that lives in the high mountains in some parts of the world. Ibexes are sure-footed and happy to climb along rocky crags. Male ibexes have long horns, which they sometimes use to fight each other.

The ten highest mountains on land are all in the Himalayas, to the north of India. The highest peak of all, Mount Everest, lies on the border between Nepal and Tibet. It is 8,863 metres high and is known to people of Tibet as Chomolongma, or "goddess mother of the world".

Rocks and Minerals

△ **White cliffs** are made of chalk. This is a type of sedimentary rock, made from the shells of tiny sea creatures.

The Earth's crust is made up of rocks, and rocks are made of one or more minerals.

There are three main kinds of rock. Sedimentary rock forms when layers of sand, mud and seashells pile up as a sediment and get squashed together. Metamorphic rock is rock that has been changed by great heat and pressure. And igneous (or "fiery") rock is made when hot, melted rock from inside the Earth cools down and goes hard.

Many of the Earth's rocks are millions of years old, but new rocks are being created all the time.

New Words

ammonite A type of shellfish that died out millions of years ago.

fossil The remains of an animal or a plant that are preserved in rock.

sediment Tiny particles that sink to the bottom of the sea and then pile up.

△ **Granite**, a strong igneous rock, was used to build the Empire State Building in New York.

◁ **Marble** is a metamorphic rock that forms when limestone is heated and squeezed. White marble is often used for sculpture.

▽ How do fossils form? Fossils are the remains of living things, such as shells or sea creatures, preserved naturally in rocks.

MAKE A LEAF FOSSIL

Roll out a layer of plasticine and press a leaf firmly into it. Then carefully remove the leaf, to leave an imprint. Make a card ring, press it into the plasticine around the imprint, and pour liquid plaster of Paris over it. When the plaster is dry, take it out, peel off the plasticine and study your leaf fossil.

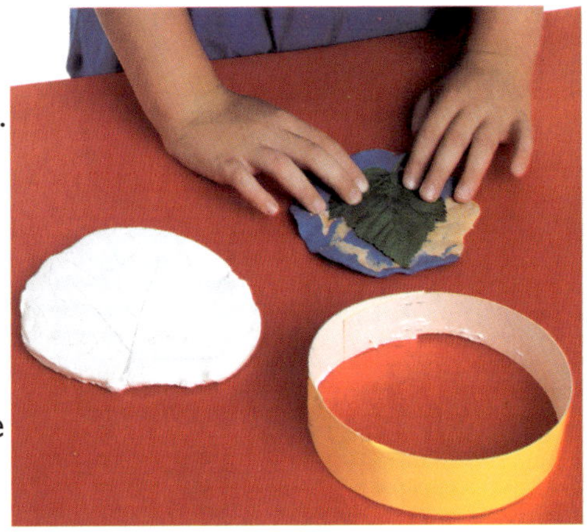

◁ Stage 1 Ammonites were sea creatures that died out about 65 million years ago. When an ammonite died, its body and coiled shell sank to the sea bed.

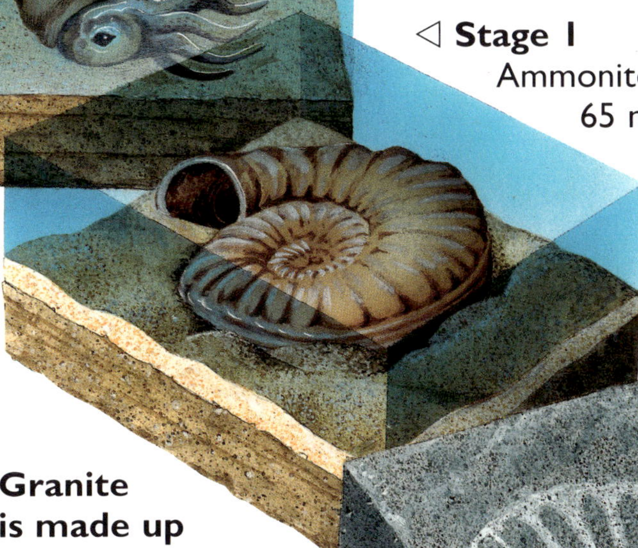

◁ Stage 2 Sediment made of sand and mud fell and built up around the ammonite. The animal's soft parts rotted, leaving just the shell.

◁ Stage 3 Over millions of years the heavy sediment hardened into rock and the ammonite's shell was replaced by minerals. This left an outline of the creature's shell inside the rock.

◁ Stage 4 Today the rock has been worn away by the weather to reveal the fossilized outline of the ammonite. Though this is not the original animal, scientists can learn a lot about the ammonite from this fossil.

Granite is made up mainly of large grains of quartz, feldspar and mica. It varies in colour from grey to red, depending on the amount of these minerals present.

▽ This beautiful mineral is called selenite. It is a kind of gypsum, which is used to make plaster of Paris, cement and school chalk.

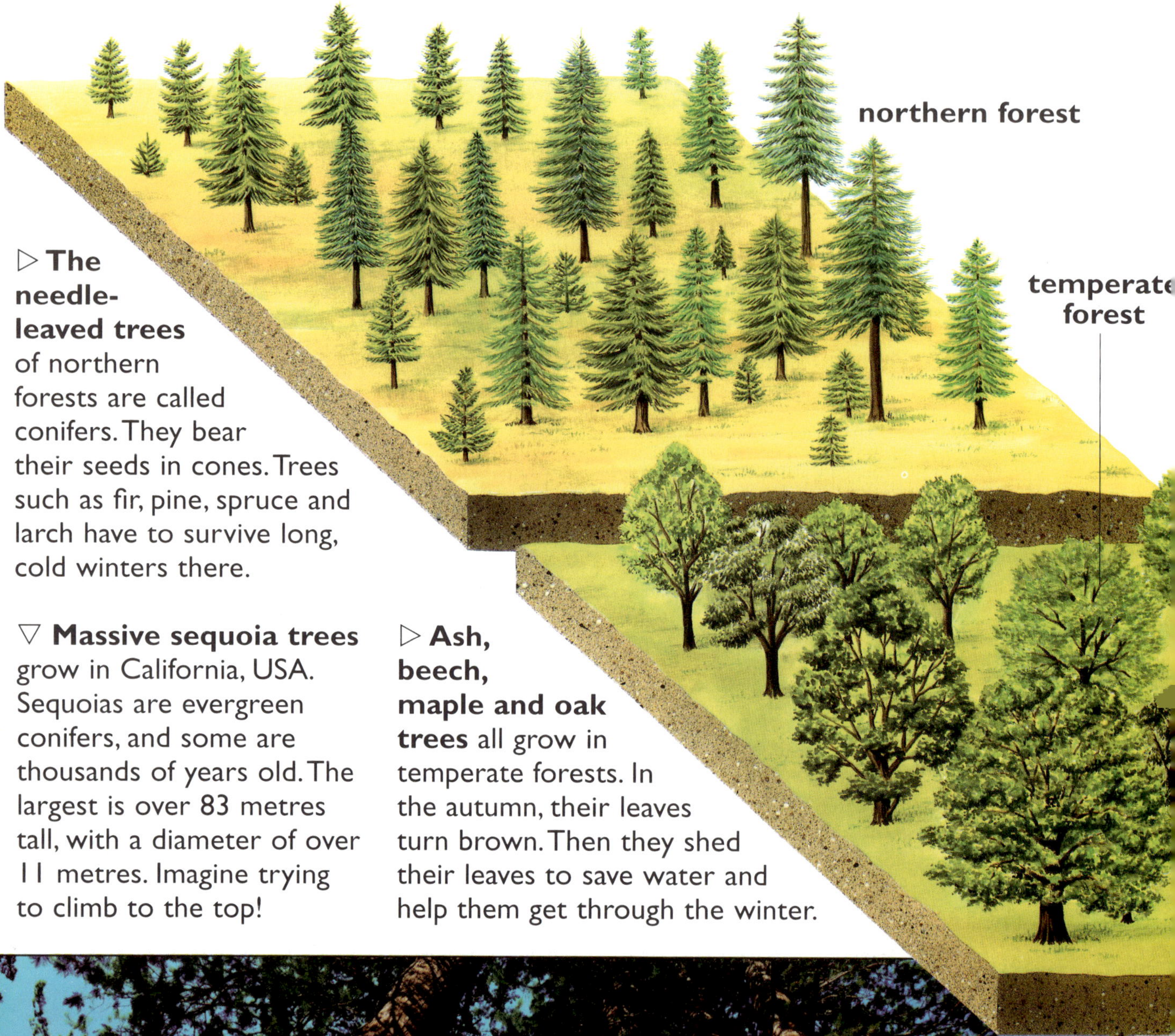

▷ **The needle-leaved trees** of northern forests are called conifers. They bear their seeds in cones. Trees such as fir, pine, spruce and larch have to survive long, cold winters there.

▽ **Massive sequoia trees** grow in California, USA. Sequoias are evergreen conifers, and some are thousands of years old. The largest is over 83 metres tall, with a diameter of over 11 metres. Imagine trying to climb to the top!

▷ **Ash, beech, maple and oak trees** all grow in temperate forests. In the autumn, their leaves turn brown. Then they shed their leaves to save water and help them get through the winter.

Forests

oak leaf

Almost a third of the Earth's land surface is covered with forests. The trees that grow in forests vary according to the region's climate – how warm it is, how long the winter lasts and how much rain falls in that region.

Cool northern forests are full of evergreen trees. Temperate forests have deciduous trees that lose their leaves in winter. And tropical rainforests have an enormous variety of big, fast-growing trees.

New Words

climate The weather conditions of an area.

conifer A tree that makes its seeds in cones.

deciduous tree A tree that loses its leaves in the autumn.

evergreen tree A tree that keeps its leaves.

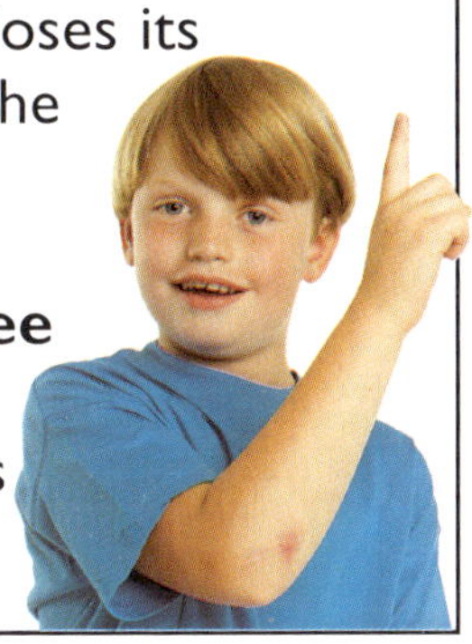

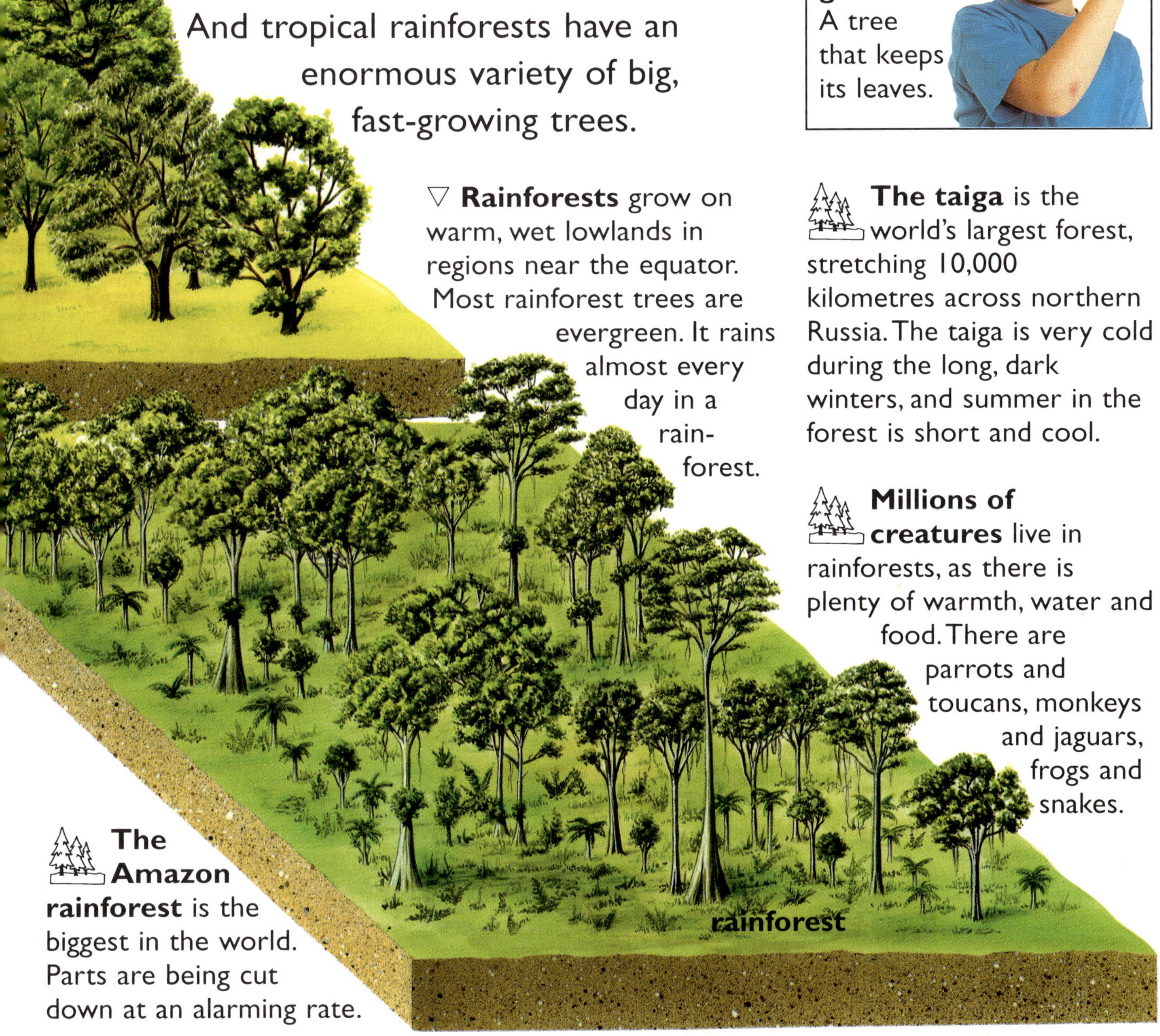

▽ **Rainforests** grow on warm, wet lowlands in regions near the equator. Most rainforest trees are evergreen. It rains almost every day in a rainforest.

The taiga is the world's largest forest, stretching 10,000 kilometres across northern Russia. The taiga is very cold during the long, dark winters, and summer in the forest is short and cool.

Millions of creatures live in rainforests, as there is plenty of warmth, water and food. There are parrots and toucans, monkeys and jaguars, frogs and snakes.

The Amazon rainforest is the biggest in the world. Parts are being cut down at an alarming rate.

Deserts

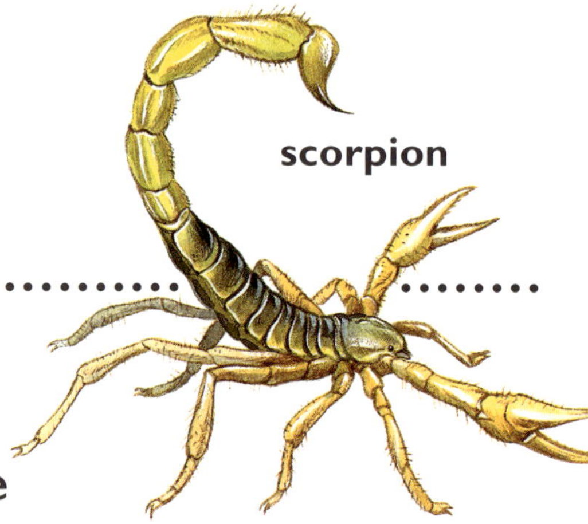
scorpion

New Words

cactus A fleshy, spiny plant that can store water.

dune A hill of sand.

oasis A place in the desert where there is water and plants can grow.

plain An area of flat country.

Most deserts are in hot parts of the world, where it is dry nearly all the time.

Some deserts are covered with huge, high sand dunes. But there are many other desert landscapes, including rocky hills and stony plains. In the world's largest desert, the Sahara in northern Africa, the temperature often reaches 50°C. Despite the heat and lack of water, these are not empty wastelands. Plants like the cactus and animals like the scorpion, and even some people, have become used to life in the desert.

Most deserts have small areas of water, where plants can grow and people can live. They are called oases. The Sahara has about 90 large oases.

▽ **In many desert regions**, rocks have been worn away over millions of years by the effects of heat and wind. The deserts of North America are full of strange-shaped, dramatic rock forms.

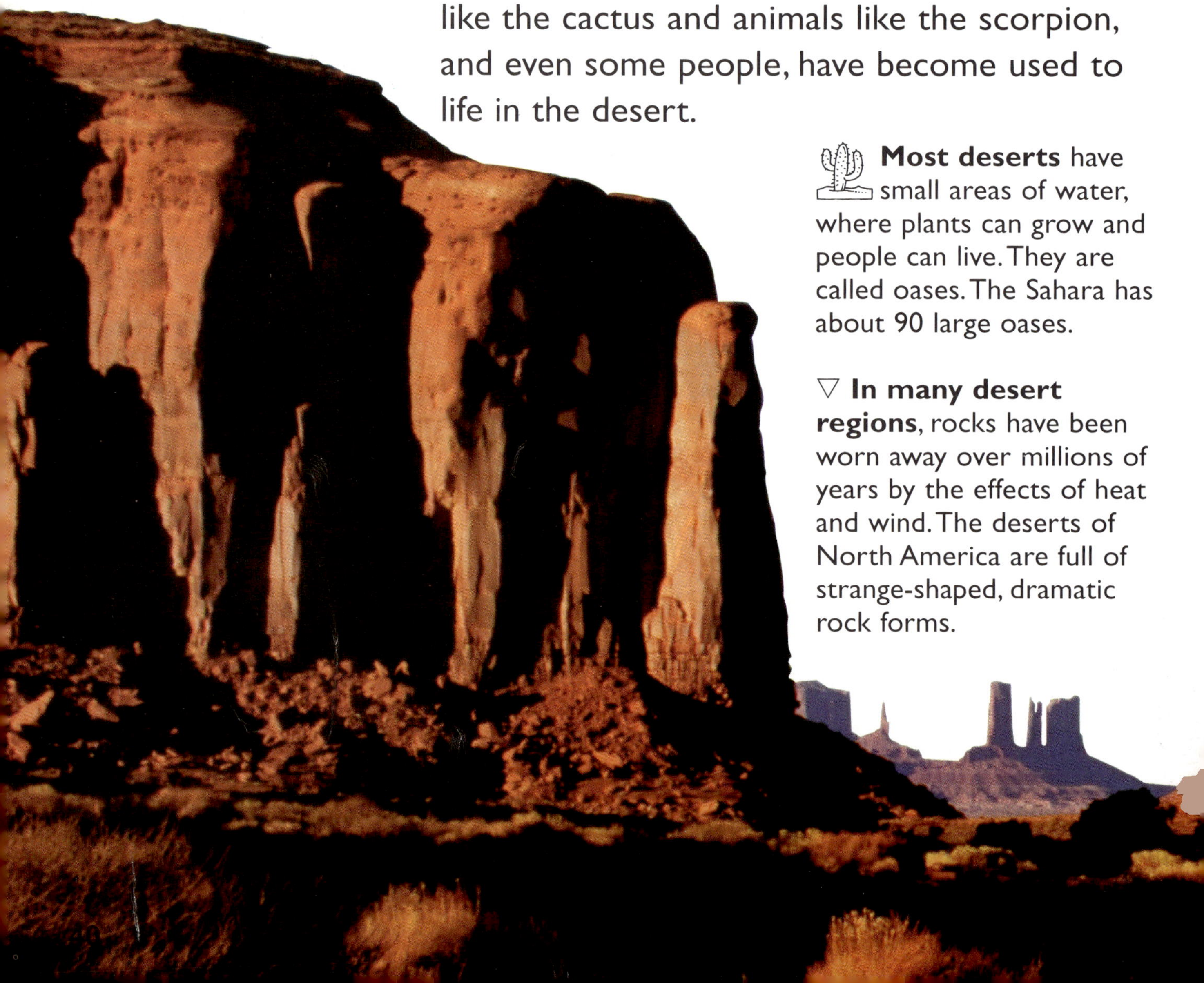

BAKING DESERT

Mix smooth dough from 6 cups of flour, 3 cups of salt, 6 tablespoons of cooking oil and water. Roll the dough and shape it into a desert landscape. Bake the desert at the bottom of the oven at a low temperature for 40 minutes. When it has cooled down, paint with PVA glue and sprinkle with sand. Paint a green oasis, and add tissue-paper palm trees and, perhaps, a plasticine camel for effect.

△ **Some of the Sahara's** sand dunes are up to 465 metres high. They are like seas of sand, and they change and drift with the action of the wind.

▷ **Cactus plants** store water in their fleshy stems. The giant saguaro cactus can grow over 17 metres tall. Other desert plants suddenly shoot up if it rains, flower quickly and scatter their seeds.

Polar Regions

▽ **There are icebergs** in the cold sea near both Poles. They are huge chunks of floating freshwater ice that break off from glaciers and ice shelves. Only about a seventh of an iceberg appears above the water, so they are much bigger than they look.

Near the North and South Poles, at the very top and bottom of the world, it is very cold.

The region around the North Pole is called the Arctic. This is a huge area of frozen sea. The Arctic Ocean is covered in thick ice, which spreads over a wider area in winter. Some Arctic people, such as the Inuit and the Lapps, live on frozen land in the north of Asia, Europe and North America.

The South Pole is on the frozen land of Antarctica, which is renowned as the coldest continent on Earth.

The largest iceberg ever seen was about 300 kilometres long and 100 kilometres wide. It was in the South Pacific Ocean.

◁ **Norwegian explorer Roald Amundsen** was first to reach the South Pole, in 1911. British explorer Robert Scott arrived a few weeks later, to find the Norwegian flag already flying there. At the South Pole, every way you look is north.

New Words

crevasse A deep crack in ice.

glacier A river of ice that moves very slowly.

iceberg A huge chunk of ice floating in the sea.

treaty A special, signed agreement between countries.

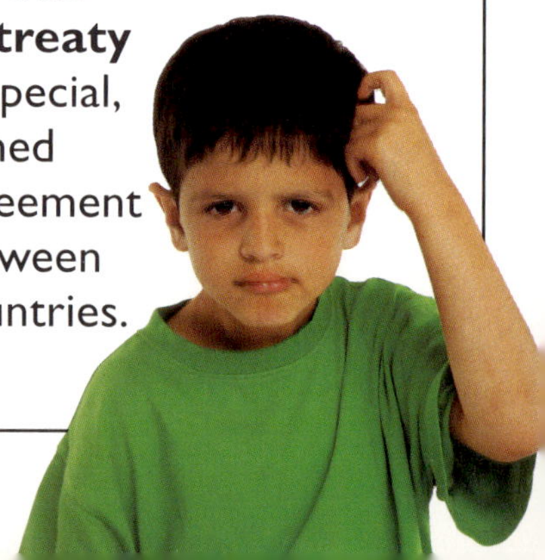

◁ **A glacier** is a mass of ice that moves slowly down a mountain like a river. As a glacier flows downhill, it often cracks into deep openings called crevasses.

In Antarctica, Lambert Glacier flows into an ice shelf, and altogether is over 700 kilometres long. Antarctica's Ross Ice Shelf is the world's largest sheet of floating ice. It is about as big as France!

▽ Working scientists are the only people who live in Antarctica. They try not to spoil the continent, which is protected by an international treaty. Greenpeace, shown here, keep a check on this. At a research station at the South Pole scientists learn about living in freezing conditions.

Saving our Planet

Many of the Earth's most beautiful areas are in danger. Oceans, seashores, forests and other regions are being overused and spoiled by people.

We can do a lot to help. Factories can stop pumping waste gases into the air and liquids into rivers. Most pollution comes from people trying to save money, instead of spending more to keep our planet clean.

△ **Some factories** pump dangerous gases into the air. These often get trapped in the atmosphere. Many scientists believe that this so-called "greenhouse effect" could be making the Earth warmer, having drastic effects on our planet.

In some parts of the world, new sources of energy are being tried out. Solar panels collect energy directly from the Sun. Wind farms use windmill generators to make electricity. The power of the oceans' waves and tides are also being used in the same way.

◁ **Drinks cans** may be crushed and recycled to make new cans. This saves energy and materials. Used glass bottles, paper and clothes, can also be collected and recycled.

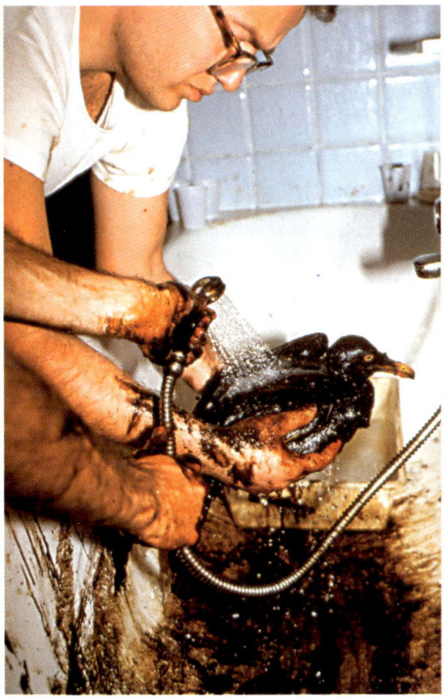

◁ **Oil spills** from huge tankers can pollute coasts. This is especially harmful to seabirds. They get clogged up with oil and then cannot fly or feed.

▷ **Fumes from factories**, power stations and car exhausts contain dangerous chemicals. Some rise into clouds and later fall as acid rain. This form of pollution can be very harmful to trees.

▽ **It's good for all** of us to plant new trees. They give out oxygen and so help make the fresh air that we need to breathe.

Leaving the car at home
Most cars run on petrol, which comes from oil. The world's oil is being used up, and car exhausts cause pollution. People can help the planet by walking and using trains and buses as much as possible.

NEW WORDS

generator A machine that makes electricity.

pollution Damage caused by poisonous and harmful substances.

recycle To change waste materials so that they can be used again.

solar panel A metal panel that collects energy from the Sun to make electricity.

Quiz

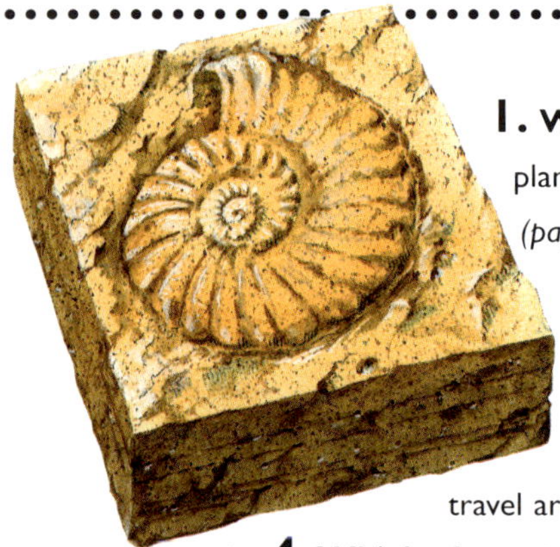

1. What is the name of the planet on which we live? *(page 8)*

2. What is a round dent in a planet's surface called? *(page 9)*

3. How many planets travel around the Sun? *(page 10)*

4. Which planet is closest to the Sun? *(page 11)*

5. Why do stars twinkle? *(page 12)*

6. The Sun is just one of thousands of millions of stars in our galaxy. What is the name of our galaxy? *(page 13)*

7. Is our Sun the hottest star in the Universe? *(page 14)*

8. Most scientists think the Universe began with a sort of explosion. What do we call it? *(page 15)*

9. When a part of the Earth is tilted towards the Sun, is it summer or winter there? *(page 16)*

10. When do leaves turn brown and start to fall from the trees? *(page 17)*

11. What is a building that houses a big telescope called? *(page 18)*

12. Can you name one famous astronomer from the past? *(page 19)*

13. In which year did humans first step onto the Moon's surface? *(page 20)*

14. Who was the first living thing to travel in space? *(page 21)*

15. What is the name of the blanket of air around the Earth? *(page 22)*

16. Is air weightless? *(page 23)*

17. The Earth's crust is cracked into huge pieces that fit together like a giant jigsaw puzzle. What are the pieces called? *(page 24)*

18. Which layer of the Earth lies just under the crust? *(page 25)*

19. Where is the world's largest active volcano? *(page 26)*

20. What is a tsunami? *(page 27)*

21. Do stalactites or stalagmites grow from the roof of a cave? *(page 28)*

22. Are the Victoria Falls in Africa or Europe? *(page 29)*

23. Which ocean covers almost half the globe? *(page 30)*

24. Which is the largest of the Earth's continents? *(page 31)*

25. What is the name for the rise and fall in the level of the sea? *(page 32)*

26. How many arms do starfish usually have? *(page 33)*

27. Is it hot or cold on high mountains? *(page 34)*

28. In which mountain range are the ten highest mountains in the world? *(page 35)*

29. What are white cliffs made of? *(page 36)*

30. What sort of animal was an ammonite? *(page 37)*

31. What sort of trees are fir, pine, spruce and larch? *(page 38)*

32. What do we call the forests that grow on warm, wet lowlands in regions near the equator? *(page 39)*

33. Most deserts have small areas with water, where plants can grow. What are these areas called? *(page 40)*

34. Where do cactus plants store water? *(page 41)*

35. Who was the first explorer to reach the South Pole? *(page 42)*

36. Where is the world's largest mass of floating ice? *(page 43)*

37. What do solar panels collect their energy from? *(page 44)*

38. Why is it good to plant new trees? *(page 45)*

Index

Acknowledgements

The publishers wish to thank the following artists who have contributed to this book:

Mike Foster (The Maltings Partnership) Page 12 (BL,T), 21 (BR), 27 (TL), 33 (BR), 35 (CR), 45 (C), caption icons throughout;
Gary Hincks 28 (T), 29 (BR), 30 (B), 35 (T), 37 (C);
Rob Jakeway 10;
Mel Pickering (Contour Publishing) 8 (BL), 9 (CL), 11 (T), 12 (C), 13 (BR), 16 (C), 19 (TR), 23 (BR), 25 (C), 30 (TL), 31 (TR);
Terry Riley 33 (T), 40 (T);
Guy Smith (Maineline Design) 14-15 (C, B), 38 (C);
Michael White (Temple Rogers) 11 (BR), 19 (L), 42 (BL).

The publishers wish to thank the following for supplying photographs for this book:

Chris Bonington Library Page 22 (B) /Doug Scott;
Miles Kelly archives 16 (BR), 17 (B), 18 (T), 27 (B), 29 (TL,TR), 30 (C), 32 (B), 34 (T, B), 36 (TL, BL, B, BR), 38 (BL), 39 (TR), 40 (B), 41 (TR, CR), 42 (C), 43 (T), 44 (TR);
PhotoDisc 8 (TL), 9 (R), 19 (B), 20 (L, B), 21 (TR), 24 (CT);
Rex Features 26 (T, BL), 43 (BR) /Greenpeace/Tim Baker, 44 (TR), 45 (TL,TR);
The Stock Market 18 (B), 23 (TR), 33 (C), 44 (BL), 45 (BR).
All model photography by **Mike Perry at David Lipson Photography Ltd.**

Models in this series:
Lisa Anness, Sophie Clark, Alison Cobb, Edward Delaney, Elizabeth Fallas, Ryan French, Luke Gilder, Lauren May Headley, Christie Hooper, Caroline Kelly, Alice McGhee, Daniel Melling, Ryan Oyeyemi, Aaron Phipps, Eriko Sato, Jack Wallace.

Clothes for model photography supplied by:
Adams Children's Wear